UNDESERVED FAVOR

RENE NICHOLAS MATLOCK

NEWMAN SPRINGS PUBLISHING
320 Broad Street
Red Bank, NJ 07701

First originally published by Newman
Springs Publishing 2024

ISBN 979-8-89308-667-6 (Paperback)
ISBN 979-8-89308-668-3 (Digital)

Printed in the United States of America

I have been driven many times to my knees
by the overwhelming conviction that I had
nowhere else to go!
—Abraham Lincoln

Introduction

My personal memoir: Living an ordinary life on earth can be fabulous when you live it with Jesus!

It is my desire, in writing my personal memoir, that all people will come to know and understand their divine purpose in life. My memoir will clearly show you that I am just an ordinary woman who learned very early in my life that *prayer* is the key to opening the door to heaven. Therefore, I want my family and future generations to have blessed lives here on earth, but the ultimate desire of my heart is that I will be with them all again in heaven for eternity!

Early Childhood

I was a child who grew up without the nurturing and love of my parents due to tragic circumstances. I was two years old when these events occurred. Therefore, I had to deal all my life with the insecurities that come from these unfortunate experiences. I don't want my story to read like "poor me," so I will skip those negative details that God has graciously healed and I have put to rest.

Note: I am now an octogenarian, which means someone who could drop dead at any moment! If we were measuring my life expectancy based on a time clock, it's midnight! So listen up, as I don't know how much time I have left on the clock to live.

I am the youngest of nine children born into an Irish family. My twin brother and I were just exactly what the family didn't need—two more mouths to feed. At a young age, my whole life changed in ways no young child would understand. My mother died, and I kept asking, "Where is Mama?" No one would answer me. My twin brother and I were passed around to live with different family members. We were finally given to two of my older sisters to raise us. They were married and had started their own families with children of their own who also needed parenting. My brother and I increased their head count from three children to five. As a child, I had no idea of the sacrifices that their families had to make for us.

While living with my sister Libby, I saw her as the "law without mercy." I viewed my other sister Anne as "mercy without the law." As strange as this must seem, I would take the law quality of Libby over Anne's *free spirit*, even though Libby was an alcoholic. Anne, who lived in chaos, drove me nuts! At age three, I would go into Anne's closet where she would throw her shoes and clothes, and I would try to match up her shoes and straighten up her mess. That closet was my sanctuary, the only place in the house where I could go, and my mind wouldn't be spinning around.

Back to the law—Libby. I will be forever grateful that she married a man who was kind and caring. What was strange was that Bob, Libby's husband, was a Navy pilot and was gone a lot on active duty. In my heart, it was Bob who I wanted to stay at home and let Libby go fight the war. If that had happened, that war would have been over in a week!

Jesus to the Rescue!

At age six, I found myself living in San Juan, Puerto Rico, where Bob had been transferred to the Navy. We had a Puerto Rican cook named Sonata who befriended me. While living in Puerto Rico, I was pretty much left to play by myself wherever I wanted because my brother had one mission in life, and that was to drive Libby crazy. He was really good at it!

One day, Sonata took me to her village. It was the first time in my life that I recognized true poverty. In the middle of all the huts in the village was an area where everyone shared in cooking their food. This is when Sonata told me about Jesus, that He was the Son of God, that He loved me, and that I was Jesus's little girl. I understood that Jesus was the Son of God, but I didn't understand that Jesus was God. She told me that even though I couldn't see Him, He could see me. And then she said that if I was ever in trouble, I needed to call on the name of Jesus to help me.

I was thrilled to know that God knew who I was and that He had sent His Son Jesus to help me live a good life and to forgive my sins. I was always looking for someone to like me—remember who I was living with!

The Scripture Romans 10:17 says,

> So faith comes from
> hearing, and hearing comes
> by the Word of God.

That means Sonata told me about Jesus, and I wanted Jesus to love me and be my friend. It was as simple as that! *I was now a Christian!*

There Is Power in the Name of Jesus!

The following paragraphs represent three different occasions when I experienced Jesus helping me in a *supernatural way*:

1. During that summer in Puerto Rico, when I was six years old, a group of friends and I were playing outside in a field. One of us noticed a bee's nest, and we did what children ages six to eight would do—we started throwing rocks and sticks at the bee's nest. Surprise! Surprise! The bees started swarming! We immediately started

running for our lives. I remembered Sonata's words, "If you are ever in trouble, call on the name of Jesus for help!" Believe me, I was yelling, "Jesus, help me!" and a voice said to me, "Fall down into the high weeds," which I did. Jesus saved me that day! I heard His voice—it would be the only time in my entire life that I would hear His voice out loud. That incident cemented my trust and faith in Jesus. As a child, I viewed my personal relationship with Him as my *good-luck charm*. Prior to this scary experience, I did not know the power in His name.

2. My second miracle was so amazing that I never told anyone until I was a grown woman because I didn't think that anyone would believe me. I was now in the second grade, and I was walking fast because I was going to

be late for school. I sure didn't want Libby to get a note from my teacher for being late to school. Suddenly, a man pulled up in his car, rolled the window down, and said, "You look like you are in a hurry. Do you want a ride?"

I said, "Yes," and got in the front seat of his car—I was naive and didn't know any better. Of course, I really did know better, but I was late for school, so I jumped in! The man then drove his car into the woods, stopped, and unzipped his pants. I immediately said, "Help me, Jesus!" After I called on Jesus for help, the man zipped up his pants and drove me back to the place where he had picked me up. He did not harm me in any way. To this day, I still get chills telling this story. Needless to say, I learned a really important and serious life lesson that day.

Psalm 116:6 says,

The Lord protects the helpless; when I was in danger, He saved me.

Thank goodness that Jesus saved me! Because of this horrible experience, I believe that it gave me a deeper understanding of the power of prayer and the power in Jesus' name, even more than most adults possess.

3. Miracle number 3 happened when I was ten or eleven years old. I was at the beach by myself, which seemed like a normal day for me. I started swimming and ended up further out in the water than I realized, and I was totally exhausted. I realized that I was too tired to make it back to shore.

Suddenly, a large wave was coming, and God provided me with a sand dune to stand on while the wave went over my head. Inside this big wave, I was able to breathe, which provided me with the air I needed in my lungs to give me the capacity to swim back to shore.

Did I understand what had just happened? No! I pondered this miracle for years before I realized that it was because of the power of prayer in *Jesus's name* that I had been saved. That simple prayer that Sonata had taught me, "Help me, Jesus!" had been heard by Him, and He answered it. I had come to Jesus with *child-like* faith, totally trusting Him! I knew at an early age that the name of Jesus had power and that I didn't! However, I did know that "I was His, and He was mine!"

These were the last three *obvious* miracles that Jesus worked in my young life. I have not experienced any other *obvious* miracles in my later years. These three miracles were important, coming at the most innocent times of my life because they cemented my trust in Jesus.

Proverbs 3:5–6 reads,

> Trust in the Lord with all your heart and do not lean on your own understanding. In all your ways acknowledge Him and He will direct your path.

Another Scripture, Hebrews 11:6, says,

> And without faith it is impossible to please God, because anyone who comes to Him must believe that He exists and that He rewards those who earnestly seek Him.

Recognizing the Power of Prayer

Now as an older lady but still a *very spry* woman, I look back at that little girl and realize that she got it right! I realize that you don't have to read the entire Bible or even open it for God to answer your prayers. You just need to know to whom you are speaking. I certainly knew nothing about the Bible or even how to read it. I prayed to Jesus with a child's heart, pure and trusting! That is what He wants from all His children from six to ninety-two years of age—a child's heart!

Praying should be as natural as breathing. You don't have to think to breathe; you just do it! I call this a *prayer truth*. This didn't come directly from the Bible, but it expresses what I learned as a child!

Prayer does not have a set of rules on how you should pray except to pray in *Jesus's name* because that is where the power comes from. You can pray on your knees, standing up, lying down, with your eyes open or shut, anytime and anywhere you choose. You can pray in your mind or out loud—you get the idea—there is no restriction on the method of prayer.

However, if you are currently an unbeliever, God is delighted to hear from you. He created you, and He knew you while you were in your mother's womb.

Jeremiah 33:3 says,

> Call to Me and I will
> answer you and tell you great
> and unsearchable things you
> do not know.

Unbelievable! God wants to have a personal relationship with you and me! The Scriptures that you will read throughout my testimony are the Scriptures that most impacted my life. And what does God want from us?

In Matthew 22:37–39, Jesus said,

> You must love the Lord your God with all your heart, all your soul, and all your mind. This is the first and greatest commandment. A second is to love your neighbor as yourself.

Why does prayer seemingly have no appeal to most people, including Christians? It is my opinion that most people are uncomfortable praying to someone they cannot see. People don't know and appreciate that God is a Spirit. This is why putting your faith in Jesus is so important.

When we take this step of faith, believing that Jesus is the Son of God, He sent us the Holy Spirit to live in our hearts to help us in our daily lives, including prayer. When we pray, the Holy Spirit and Jesus are interceding to God the Father for us so that our prayers are properly communicated and received by God! Prayer is the most powerful gift that God has given us. It is our vehicle to communicate directly with Him!

I have and will continue to share personal memories of my life that I hope you find interesting—but they will not change or influence your life. Only the Word of God and the Holy Spirit can do that. My current family members and my future generation family members who read this testimony need to understand that without Jesus as your foundation, you really have no real purpose in this life. Having a personal relationship with Jesus provides you and me hope and a future!

It's my prayer that all of you will have a desire to read and study God's Word, the Bible.

Luke 24:45 says,

> Then He opened their
> minds to understand Scripture.

Prayer Truth: Probably up until now, Satan has left you alone because you have not been seeking Jesus, but once you do, "the battle will begin!" Satan will not let loose of you easily when you are seeking a personal relationship with Jesus Christ. Satan understands that your current view of the world without Jesus Christ is, "Is this all that I will ever have?" Your complete mindset is just as William Henley wrote in his poem, "I am the master of my fate, I am the captain of my soul."

Satan at Work

Question: Can Satan cause hate to enter the heart of a child?

Of course. At nine years old, when I was still living with Libby, I watched my twin brother helping to make Libby into an even bigger alcoholic than she already was. Then Libby came to my room during the night and woke me up to inform me that in the morning I would be getting on an airplane and flying to Texas, where I would now be living with Anne. I didn't sleep very well the rest of that night!

My heart was so full of anger toward my twin brother that I didn't even remember saying goodbye to him. In my little girl heart, I couldn't understand why I was being sent away and Ronnie was getting to stay with Libby. I didn't realize that Libby was being kind to Anne by not sending Ronnie as well. I didn't understand that the two of us, plus her own children, were taking up all of Libby's time and ultimately her life. She didn't want to pass this same load and responsibility on to Anne, so she kept Ronnie. I didn't see Ronnie again for several years. As far as I was concerned, he was dead! Satan had won a big battle in my life, causing me to hate my brother!

However, I did see him off and on through the latter years of his life. He was such a mess. The only time I would hear from him was when he needed money. Most of my friends didn't even know that I had a brother. I did go to see him shortly before he died, and we had a good conversation. He assured me that he had asked Jesus to come into his heart as his Lord and Savior! It gives me a lot of peace knowing that Ronnie, that little boy who was adorable but needed love, was by God's grace in heaven.

My New Home Address

I was now living in never-never land with Anne. Living in Anne's chaos was very diffi-cult for me—remember that little three-year-old girl in Anne's closet trying to match her shoes together? The years spent with Anne were amazing to me. *No rules. Period!* Anne's husband, Pete, was a wonderful man, but he too was an alcoholic. He was kind and had his own company. Some years we lived very, very well, but then something would hap-pen, and the big cars would disappear along with some other things. Then Pete would get himself back together again, and we would be back in never-never land again!

So what did I learn from this experience? People were much nicer when we were climbing up the ladder than when we were coming down. I immediately understood there was a divide between the *have-nots* and those that *have*! At a very young age, I understood this sad but very true *truth*.

How interesting it is that our Lord and Savior chose the *have-nots* as His disciples to go out and change the world! Money is not evil, but the love of it over people is!

Sweet, kind, wonderful, beautiful Anne. We all felt this way, and so did she! Anne would live in her own world, which she had created in her mind. She believed that she was Scarlett O'Hara. There were absolutely no rules in Anne's house, and it was a complete wreck. Just consider me to be the live-in maid. Remember, I am the one who has problems with chaos—just call me Cinderella.

However, Anne was good to me, so I put her on a pedestal. During my life, I put several people on a pedestal. The problem was that they were humans with flaws, just like I am a human with flaws. I now understand why Jesus alone is to be worshiped.

Children need security, and that was a feeling that I would fight for my whole life. Everyone I had lived with had their own children, and of course, their own children would come first!

Prayer Truth: If I only had one message to leave behind, it would be this: *the greatest gift you can give your child is that they would love Jesus more than anyone else, including you.* I say this because when Ronnie and I were separated, I learned that people will forsake and leave you. I never understood how anyone could separate twins.

Jesus said in Hebrews 13:5, "Never will I leave you," and "Never will I forsake you!"

My life again would experience a big shock and a major change. Pete would die in a freak truck accident without leaving a will.

What to do about his company? What about other assets? Anne would hire lawyers to help, but by the time everything got resolved, the lawyers were the only ones who came out on top!

I learned some life lessons from watching Pete's business go up and down financially and realizing that he had ultimately left Anne with nothing after his death. I developed a good work ethic as a babysitter and learned to save my money. At sixteen, I got a full-time job during the summer and then added a second job during the holidays. That job was working at a retail store, and I worked in the hosiery department.

My next job was working for Marjorie Rebushay, an older French woman, but still beautiful. She had black hair, blue eyes, and a thick French accent. She owned a credit collection company that contacted people who had not paid their bills with *dire* circumstances if they didn't pay up! She also kept a bottle of bourbon in the top right-hand drawer. Here I was with another alcoholic. I loved her accent; she would say, "Please close the vanishing blinds" instead of "venetian blinds." If a client was cordial, she would say he was congealed. I even received a telephone call from a man asking for Mrs. Rubbershoes.

The reason she hired me was because of my name. My name is spelled Renee on my birth certificate. However, in the fourth grade, I decided to drop an "e" in my official name, not realizing that *Rene* was the boy's version. I tell you this so you can see a little bit of the pure Irish in me. I never did tell Mrs. Rebushay.

I then worked for a German oil company—four men and me! One of these men took care of my income taxes, another one took care of my car, and they all contributed to my well-being in one way or another.

It was during this time frame that I would meet my husband. My friend and I shared an apartment because we couldn't afford to live alone. She was beautiful Bonnie, and I was the little five-foot-two redhead, Rene. I certainly wasn't in the same league as her if we were to enter a beauty contest. However, I had no lack of self-confidence and no shortage of boyfriends. The funniest thing was that *beautiful Bonnie* would date jerks who weren't kind to her. She told me that she was only interested in dating men who were or would be rich!

It was Christmas, and we were attending a party together. I still remember my outfit—a silver beaded dress that flowed to my knees. For you women reading this, the dress had a 1920s look, accompanied by silver heels with glass buckles. I was looking good!

I think you could safely assume that Bonnie and I were not looking for a man of character, integrity, and honor. We were looking for tall, dark, and handsome, with a sports car and an associated lifestyle. Isn't this the way the world thinks? *Yes!*

The door opened, and in walked my dream man—six-foot-one-inch of handsome. He had dark hair, blue eyes, and I immediately knew that this was the one! I only had one problem: I was standing next to *beautiful Bonnie*. We had previously made an agreement that whoever "Mr. Tall, Dark, and Handsome" called on the phone or asked one of us for a date, the other person would back away. Did I think I had a chance against *beautiful Bonnie*? Of course not! I just acted like I did. To my astonishment, David Nicholas— *he even had a beautiful name*—came directly over to me. Hallelujah! Hallelujah!

Things moved quickly, and we ultimately got married, having a beautiful wedding. After we got married, David still had six months to serve in the military before he would be discharged. We were now living in Cape May, New Jersey. During the winter, this little town would be empty, but in the summer, it was robust and the place to go—a wonderful resort and vacation town. The problem for us was that we arrived during the winter, and there were no jobs. The only job available was a teller position at a branch bank near the beach.

I went to the main bank, filled out an application, and they hired me. Of course, they would; my application made me sound like I could run the bank. I was confident that my previous boss would give me a good reference.

You need to understand that I had this little thing with numbers—they just twirled around in my head. My calculator had saved my life more than once. So the fact that I couldn't count to twenty without using my fingers and toes—was I worried about working in a bank? Of course not! I thought to myself, *How hard can this be? I will just watch everything going on around me and do as others do. Just call me naive!*

Mr. Temple was my boss. I know you will find this hard to believe, but I was there only five minutes, looking at my money drawer, when I heard a man's voice calling for Mrs. Nicholas. He repeated it, "Mrs. Nicholas," and then he patted me on my shoulder. I was a new bride, and no one had called me Mrs. Nicholas before, so I didn't realize he was calling me. He asked me to follow him to his office. I was to sit in the chair directly in front of his desk. I could tell he was a little agitated; his face was red, and he was leaning over his desk. He then asked me, "Why did you lie on your application?" and then he asked me, "Have you ever even been in a bank?"

I told the truth, "I needed a job!" I told him that my husband was in the military and that we would only be in Cape May for six months. This is where being cute and young with a husband in the military would pay off.

Plus, Mr. Temple had a daughter my age. I didn't realize it, but God was growing my prayer life and showing me His grace! I had to assure Mr. Temple several times that I indeed would be gone in six months. It goes without saying Mr. Temple is now one of my life's heroes.

I loved working at the bank. All the old men owning the various motels along the shore used our bank, and I developed friendships with them. They were always wanting to give me money for a Coke or a cup of coffee. Yes, I had enough sense not to take a penny. I only got in trouble once with a customer who always insisted on *clean* money. One day, when we were extremely busy, in walked the *clean-money man*. Why didn't he go to one of the other tellers? So I did his transaction and gave him the cleanest money I had in my drawer. He insisted that the money was dirty! So I told the *clean-money man* to take the money and go home and wash it! None of the other tellers said a word to me—they must have had encounters of their own with the *clean-money man*!

My six months of employment at the bank were up, and they gave me a going-away party. I am sure that if I see any of them in heaven, they will be wearing a crown with jewels because of their kindness to me.

My prayer map would now really grow, and again, I was completely unaware that God's grace was working in my life. We did have Dave's G.I. Bill, which he used, but it was certainly not enough money to meet our needs. I needed to get another job! I would be the working wife subsidizing our income while Dave was getting his degree at Penn State.

You guessed it, I was filling out an application to get a job at Penn State. I was hoping to work in either the History or English departments, but there were no openings in either of these departments. The person conducting the job interviews at Penn State felt that she had the perfect job for me. Mr. Temple must have given me quite a good rec-ommendation. He was probably worried that I might want to come back to the bank!

God must have been showing me that He has a sense of humor. I got the job, and I was now the secretary for the Assistant Head of Mathematics at Penn State University. My new boss and I hit it off well. This would be my favorite all-time job! I got to boss around all the PhDs—yes, me, the one who could not count to twenty without using her fingers and toes!

The goodness of the Lord allowed me to experience university life right along with Dave. Dave got to experience faculty life because we were invited for dinner. Now that brings back the memory of eating my first artichoke, and I had no idea how to attack it. So I watched the other people present and did what they did—peeling off a leaf, dipping it in butter, and eating a small amount of meat at the end of the leaf until I finally found the heart of the artichoke. In my humble opinion, the process it takes to eat an artichoke is not worth all the work!

Now I will give you a few of the many wonderful highlights that we experienced at Penn State. We never missed a Penn State home football game. Dave's attitude was if they can play in this weather, then we can sit in it. Therefore, we would watch the entire football game, no matter how cold, how much rain, or what the score was!

We made lifelong friends there and would take day trips together with barely enough money to buy a meal. We didn't care; life was wonderful! We would never miss anything that was free on campus, including wrestling—that should speak to how desperate we were for something to do. We would often fill our car up with gasoline with friends who helped to pay for the gas and go exploring—trips to New York or to the Amish communities while visiting all the small towns in between.

These years passed by so quickly. Dave graduated from Penn State with honors, achieving an architectural engineering degree. Dave's family came from Wales and had come to America for a better life. I can still remember how proud his grandmother was of him graduating from Penn State! She wore a blue dress with a brooch, a white hat, and gloves to his commencement ceremony. She looked just like the Queen Mum!

Dave later accepted a job with an engineering firm in Houston, Texas. Dave was very involved in a palace project in the Middle East; it even had a waterfall in the palace. However, a major mistake was made in the design of the palace restrooms. All the commodes were facing Allah, and they had to be turned to face the other direction. A man could not be facing Allah when he was taking a *tinkle*!

Dave was involved in all sorts of construction projects, from designing churches to office buildings, including buildings in the Houston Medical Center, but his specialty was airports. There were not many airport projects that Dave wasn't responsible for designing various aspects of the airport, everything from runways to the train that transported passengers from terminal to terminal, and everything in between. He was also retained periodically as a consultant to other firms that needed his expertise—not only in the United States but around the world, such as in Japan, the Middle East, and Mexico! Dave was highly respected in his industry. Dave advanced in management and became the youngest vice president in the company and later became a partner! Dave was a man of few words and had a very humble spirit. He was honored throughout his life and received many awards for his architectural/engineering work, including special recognition in Washington, D.C. for a federal government project that he managed. I was very proud of him!

Only once in my life did I have to take a stand for Christ where a bad outcome could happen. Dave and I were in Quebec, Canada, at an airport convention. That night at dinner, along with Dave's boss and his wife, we were sitting with several other couples. Suddenly, I was put in a situation that I never expected. I had no idea how the subject of religion even came up—certainly not from me. Then a Muslim man sitting across from me made this statement, "We all serve the same God." I knew that I had to respond and give the correct answer, but I was concerned in my mind that my answer could cost Dave his job! I responded to the Muslim man's statement by saying, "I respectfully disagree. My God's name is not Allah. My God's name is Jesus!"

Then there was dead silence. Dave said in a quiet voice, "I agree with Rene." Instead of something bad happening, Dave received a job promotion. Thank You, Jesus!

David Nicholas was the first person in my life to really love me, and I knew that I was number one in his life. What wife could ask for anything more than for her husband to love and fully respect her?

When we would travel on trips, he would tell me about the various buildings that we would see and, more importantly, the ones that he felt were worthy for me to know about. I thought he was a genius, and he thought I was adorable and funny! He felt secure enough with me to show the type of English humor he possessed, which, when he shared it, would cause him to roll around on the floor in laughter! Dave saw things in me that I did not see in myself! He felt like I was smart and accomplished. I will be forever grateful for his encouragement!

Did we have disagreements? Of course, we did—many times! But we both realized that it was better to forgive and forget them!

Wanting to Start a Family

We really wanted to start a family, but I had a miscarriage while I was working at Penn State. So after we moved to Houston, I decided to get a job to keep busy and to keep my mind from thinking about it. Get ready! Here it comes! I decided to apply for a job at Rice University. Once again, I wanted to be in the History or English departments. Unfortunately, all they had open was an opportunity in the Biochemistry department. I told them, "No, thank you!" I decided that I would just go and apply for a job at the University of Houston.

Later that evening, something truly amazing happened! There was a knock at our door, and much to my surprise, there stood the two people who had interviewed me earlier that day about a job at Rice University, which I had turned down. They were following up on our earlier meeting that day and offered me the same job opportunity, but this time, they offered to pay me more money, plus give me season tickets to all the home football games. I didn't realize at that time that only about a dozen people showed up at the Rice football games. I accepted the job!

Then I turned, and for the only time in my life, I asked David, "Tell me, David, has anything like this ever happened to you?" He just stood there with a big smile on his face!

This proved to be another spiritual growth period for me in recognizing God's sovereignty and the way He was blessing my life. It proved to be a good experience for me while I was working at Rice University.

However, while I was working there, I had several more miscarriages, plus I had major surgery which enabled me to have the ability to carry a baby. My peers were so sweet and caring, even putting a box under my feet to make me more comfortable during my pregnancy. Many afternoons, an ice cream cone would be given to me. What precious memories I have of working at Rice University!

We had just bought our first home on David's G.I. Bill. It was built in a subdivision out in the middle of nowhere on land that had previously been an old rice paddy. In our new garage stood my prized possession, a washer and dryer. To me, it was like having a diamond ring!

I was now in my ninth month of pregnancy. I was planning to work at Rice University as long as I could because I wanted to buy Dave a lawnmower to mow our yard, which had no grass! I knew that I was going to have a cesarean section, so I knew the last day that I would be able to work. My coworkers gave me a surprise baby shower. Again, God had placed me with wonderful people, and a few of them would become long-term friends. On my last day, I was waiting for my final paycheck while other paychecks were being passed out to everyone else, and I didn't get a check. Boy, was I mad! My hormones took over; I was so upset! I didn't realize that Rice University required an exit interview with everyone leaving the university. This was the way that they made sure that you would attend the exit meeting—they would hold your final paycheck. My concern was that I was going to miss the lawnmower sale at Sears. My boss was kind and offered to go buy the lawnmower for me. So I waddled over to a building to get my final paycheck. The building where the exit interview was to take place seemed to me like it was five miles away considering my condition. I walked in and said, "Just look at me, and you can guess why I am leaving." I got my final paycheck and went directly to Sears and bought the lawnmower for Dave!

Prince Charming Was Born!

Okay, Jason, I am going to tell you the truth! I was in the hospital sharing a room with another woman. We both would have our babies on the same day. They brought her baby in first, and she started telling everyone how beautiful her baby was. Well, I was waiting patiently for my *prince charming* to arrive…and you were screaming your head off! The nurses had put some drops in your eyes, which you did not appreciate! Then they put you in my arms, and I looked at you. You were bright red from being so mad, you had one eye shut, and your hair stood straight up in the air! I held you close and felt love and joy like I had never felt before in my life! This is exactly what I was thinking: I don't care how you look; *I love you!* Just so you know, the next day your face, eyes, and hair were perfect. You indeed were my *prince charming*!

You were and will always be the love and joy of my heart! You were a really funny child! One memory I have—and I don't remember why—was that I told you that you were going to get a licking for something. However, I do remember your response to my threat! You were around three years old, and you looked up at me and asked, "So who is going to spank you?" *I immediately asked God to please let me be smarter than a three-year-old!*

Jason, you were adorable then, and you still are today! Your dad and I both realized how exceptionally intelligent you were, also possessing practical common sense. We also recognized what a good athlete you were! You played every sport which had a ball in it! I also remember how daring you were riding a skateboard—I was a nervous wreck!

We carpooled with other mothers in taking our children to school. I think you were in the second grade when this happened. One of the other boys in the carpool was able to memorize all the spelling words for that week just on the way home that day. After he got out of the car, you looked at me and said, "He's smart, but I am well-rounded!" Again, in the second grade, your teacher pulled me aside and told me that she had asked you if you had done such and such. She said that you informed her that you had not done what she was asking about because you had integrity! I was so proud of you!

Then in the fourth grade, your teacher put you in charge of the class while she was gone for a short time. By the time she returned, there was an uproar going on in class. You had written on the blackboard the names of the classmates who had gotten out of their seats or said something that you didn't like. *Then if they complained about you writing their names on the blackboard, you would add a checkmark beside their names!*

I always resented the notion that only children were spoiled. I was married to an only child, and he was wonderful! We could take you with us anywhere and everywhere, and you were always well-mannered. I hope that you have good memories of our visits with family, our family vacations, and trips that we took to various countries in Europe. One day, while we were visiting the Louvre Museum in Paris, you astonished your dad and me when you saw a large painting of Napoleon being crowned king and you knew the whole story behind it!

On our trip to Wales, we visited relatives and saw the house where your beloved grandfather was born. As you remember, the valley behind his house is where the British hid the

Americans before they invaded Normandy. Four of your great-uncles fought in that war.

It was in London where you began your collection of miniature English soldiers. We also made trips to Paris and Holland. Do you remember visiting Anne Frank's house? Then we went to the city of Haarlem to Corrie Ten Boom's house, where you stood in the opening that was cut out in the wall where they hid the Jewish people during the war. The Spirit of God could be felt in this small house.

Building the Right Foundation!

Another fond memory of mine is that, before you went to school each morning, we would read from your children's Bible and then say a prayer. I knew from my own experience that without Jesus, you would be vulnerable to the threats and temptations of this world! My mindset was that I wanted you to be a "man of God" and to depend on Jesus for direction in your life. The greatest protection that any of us could have for our children is to let Jesus lead them!

Proverbs 22:6 says,

> Train up a child in the way he should go, even when he is old, he will not depart from it.

Did I do everything right? As every parent will tell you, no! Now in my old age, I look back and think how ironic it is that the wisdom I have now is what I really needed as a wife and mother back then! We all wish that we could have do-overs, but life doesn't work like that! However, I do know someone who does "makeovers," and His name is Jesus Christ!

Romans 8:28 says,

> For we know that all things work together for good to those who love God and to those who are called according to His purpose.

Prayer Truth: This does not mean that everything that happens to us is good. Evil is prevalent in our world today, but God can turn around bad circumstances for our long-range good!

We all need to start our day with Jesus in prayer and in studying His Word, the Bible, even if it is for only fifteen minutes. Would you go out your front door naked? No, we must all put on the full armor of God and dress ourselves and our family members. Remember, Satan is alive and well on planet Earth and wants to destroy you! The greatest weapon you will ever have against Satan is God's Word! The good news for us is that when we read the last chapter of the Bible… *WE WIN!*

Therefore, dress yourself with the full armor of God:

1. Put on the belt of truth.
2. Put on the breastplate of righteousness.

3. Wear shoes that take you in peace wherever He sends you.
4. Carry the shield of faith that fights off the darts of Satan.
5. Wear the helmet of salvation—think as Jesus thinks! "What Would Jesus Do?" (WWJD)
6. Wield the sword of the Spirit—*the Word of God!*

Father-and-Son Time Playing Golf

Jason, you were growing up, and your father was more involved in your life. He never missed anything that you were involved in unless he was out of town. One of my favorite memories is when he would take you to play golf with him. You were either eleven or twelve years old. One time when you guys got home from playing golf, you informed me that your dad had said "a bad word" sixteen times during that round of golf. Of course, I went into the bathroom where your dad was taking a shower and admonished him! Your dad yelled back to me from the shower, "That was only one bad word for each hole!" Then I went back to you and admonished you for telling on your dad! Then I said to you, "If that is the worst word that you ever hear, then you need to get on your knees and thank God!"

It really amazed your dad that all through the years when you guys played golf together, you were just enjoying playing golf for fun and having a good time just being with your dad! He said that you had natural ability for playing golf and that you were a very good little golfer! Your dad said that you were a much better golfer than he would ever be!

Growing Spiritually

One day I was ironing—today, this is a really lost art—so I turned on the radio and heard this person who sounded like a *country hick*. His name was J. Vernon McGee. The radio program was entitled "Five Years Through the Bible with J. Vernon McGee." He was my first Bible teacher. At this time in my life, I didn't realize that the *King James Version* of the Bible wasn't the only translation of the Bible.

My neighbor was the first person I had ever met who quickly let me know that she was a Christian. I was always told that you don't discuss politics and religion in a public setting. I was intrigued by her! She seemed like a normal person. One day she came to visit me with a gift; it was *The Living Bible*. *Wow*! It was a much easier Bible for me to read and understand. She became another one of my lifelong friends!

You might wonder why I don't use people's names. It's because I'm much older now, and I have also had a mini-stroke! So I don't want any of my friends to think that I have forgotten their names! The only name that I want you to remember is Jesus*!*

I was now ironing less and listening more to J. Vernon McGee, plus reading my new Bible. I was now praying that Dave would want Jesus in his life like I did. At this point in our marriage, we had not stepped one foot into a church. Unfortunately, I was driving Dave away from Jesus by pushing him and not leading him to Him! What to do? What to do?

Late one night, because of the joy in my heart from having received Jesus as my Lord and Savior and because of my newfound understanding of the Bible, I decided it was time to inform Dave that he was going to *hell* if he didn't believe that Jesus was the Son of God and that He was the Savior of the world. Dave informed me that he believed me and that because of me, Hell wasn't looking too bad!

I remember Dave's exact words: "I am happy that you found Jesus! That's *wonderful.* Now just leave me alone!"

Then I heard Jesus's voice, not out loud, but in my mind: "Rene, be quiet!" I was stunned and sat down on the couch. *So you might ask me how I knew that it was the voice of God.* Because such a thought would have never entered my mind!

Jason was now two years old and sleeping in his *big boy* bed. He had never gotten up out of his bed before, but that night, he came into the living room. He walked right up to his dad and said, "Daddy, Jesus is coming!"

Dave looked at me and said, "How did you make him say that?"

Dave could tell by looking at me that I was shocked! It took a long, long time for me to understand what God was saying to me: "Rene, I don't need your help! I can wake up a two-year-old boy from his sleep to achieve my purpose!"

Prayer Truths: There are over twenty-eight times in the Bible that God tells us who He is. Isaiah 45:5 says, "I am the Lord, there is no other God." God has every right to claim you as His own. He created you! Jeremiah 1:5 says, "Before I formed you in your mother's womb, I knew you; before you were born, I set you apart."

How amazing! Long before you and I were born or even conceived, He knew us and had a plan for our lives. Whenever you feel discouraged or inadequate, remember God has always thought of you as valuable and has a distinct purpose and plan for your life!

I have often wondered why the world gets so angry when Christians proclaim that

Jesus is the only living God and that He is the only way to get into heaven! There are many religions in the world and all their gods are dead: Allah, Mohammed, Buddha, and others. Jesus is the only true and living God who can save you! All the other gods want you to die for them, but Jesus died for us!

> Jesus says, "I am the way,
> the truth, and the life, and
> no one can go to the Father
> except by me." (John 14:6)

Prayer Truth: There will be things that will happen that you will never be able to understand this side of heaven. This is where a person's faith comes into play. Remember, God is sovereign and in complete control. God doesn't hold us accountable for what we don't know, but He does hold us accountable for what we do know!

Here is something that I have never understood! When something bad happens to someone or someone dies, people ask, "Why did God let this happen?" Or "I am never going to believe in God again!" and, "I'm going to stop going to church!" These people never blame Satan for bad things! Have you ever heard these people curse Satan?

Prayer Truth: Satan will always be whispering in your ear that you don't need to confess your sins or ask for forgiveness from God for a sin you committed. Nor does he want you to tell someone that you might have hurt and that you are sorry and ask for their forgiveness. When you let Satan influence and control your life, he has got you! Satan knows that if you sincerely confess your sins to God, He will be faithful and will forgive and forget them! You will have been set free by the *blood* of the Lamb!

There have been many times in my life when I have been guilty of being a hypocrite because I had not quickly confessed to a particular sin that I committed! I am so grateful that the Holy Spirit will convict me of a sin so I can immediately ask God to forgive me, in Jesus's name! I ask the Holy Spirit to never let my sin grow from one inch to a foot in length! I want to confess that sin and receive His forgiveness immediately!

If you don't understand how the Holy Spirit works, then let me make it very easy for you to understand. Here is an analogy: When you are driving a car and you are approaching a traffic light. If the light turns *green*, you go. If it turns *yellow*, you slow down, and if it turns *red*, you stop! This is exactly how the Holy Spirit works! When you get the red light in your mind, you don't do or go there! Don't do anything until the Holy Spirit has turned that light in your heart and mind from red to green!

Jason was growing older, and I was now attending a Bible-believing church in Houston, Texas. I thought to myself that God had a real challenge on His hands dealing with Dave's lack of spirituality. I shared with Dave that if he didn't go to church with me, then Jason wouldn't want to go either. *Surprise! Surprise!* It turned out that I was the real challenge for God! I was the one who would have to change my approach to dealing with this issue. No longer was I to be Dave's *spiritual advisor*. I was to show Dave God's great love without speaking a word. Wow! Didn't God know that I was Irish? Well, as we all know, actions speak louder than words!

I started doing little things for Dave that I knew he would appreciate without saying a word. I would serve him hot tea at night while he was working in his home office. Remember, he was Welsh, and they love hot tea! I stopped saying anything about going with me to church. I just continued to do what the Holy Spirit put on my heart as nice gestures for Dave.

Our church was having a revival, and I asked Dave if he would like to attend the revival with me. At this point, I wasn't hounding him to death! He said yes! I was thrilled; I had never attended a revival.

During the revival, the pastor asked the congregation if there were any families willing to host some of the speakers and their wives. I started to raise my hand, and Dave gave me the "no" look, but up went my hand anyway! (I failed to mention to you that I am a *redhead*.) Not only did we host the head speaker and his wife, but the speaker had worked as an engineer earlier in his life. Unbelievable! How many pastors do you know who had previously worked as an engineer? Only God could have arranged this! That very weekend, Dave accepted Jesus as his personal Lord and Savior. Thank You, Lord!

I have many people in my family who do not understand what being saved means (salvation).

1 Corinthians 2:14 says,

> A man who is not a
> Christian cannot understand
> the thoughts of God which
> the Holy Spirit teaches that
> it is foolish to him.

Please listen carefully: God does not exhibit Himself to you—God exhibits Himself in you! The Holy Spirit comes into a person's life and changes them the moment that person accepts Jesus Christ as their personal Lord and Savior.

Prayer Truths: One of Satan's primary purposes is to keep a person from having a personal relationship with Jesus Christ.

> Be self-controlled and
> alert, your enemy the devil
> prowls around like a roaring

lion looking for someone to devour. (1 Peter 5:8)

Resist the devil, and he will flee! (James 4:7)

Years would pass, and Dave and I were both growing in our faith through prayer and Bible study. I started attending an international Bible study, which I continued to attend, off and on, for approximately forty years. God gave me various spiritual assignments in serving Him during this time. My prayer life was growing not only through my Bible study but also through God putting other prayer warriors in my life. These were Christian women who mentored me in the faith. Throughout my life, I have had many "sisters in Christ" who truly represented "Jesus with skin on" and who would join me in various prayer groups.

In church, I was given opportunities to serve in ways that I never dreamed would happen to me. In the international Bible study organization that I attended, I was selected to serve in various leadership roles. Please believe me when I say that the next statement I am about to share can happen to you: *Self-pride* can cause a person to seek personal recognition instead of dying to oneself and giving God complete glory for any accomplishments. I missed out on several opportunities for leadership because I was enjoying the accolades that were being given to me too much. I recognized this problem in my spirit (pride), so I turned down the proposed promotions in leadership. God will test you to ensure that you are selflessly serving Him. If not, He will remove you from that service.

I was so ashamed and embarrassed with myself when the Holy Spirit convicted me of this pride in my heart that I immediately confessed it, repented, and He restored me. Thank You, Jesus!

The little home that we lived in on the rice paddy provided many wonderful memories of watching Jason grow up from being a baby to a ten-year-old. He was really involved in sports and skateboarding! He and his friends would build ramps that looked like mountains to me! I am happy to report that he is still alive!

Jason loved the Fourth of July parade. The kids would decorate their bikes for the parade and ride up and down the street. The dads would set up their barbeque grills around the cul-de-sac. One particular Fourth of July was very special. Military friends of ours came to visit us and brought fireworks to add to the celebration. One of them had some very old ammunition in the trunk of his car and couldn't wait to add this *ammo* to the evening celebration! He put it all in a bucket in our front yard. Did I know what was about to happen? No! I thought that he was a mature adult who had some common sense. He didn't! We no longer had a front yard… We now just had a bunker! Aren't memories wonderful! Jason said that it was the best Fourth of July ever!

Family Moving to Austin, Texas

We would now be making a major life change. Dave had been promoted to vice president and became a partner of the firm. His promotion required us to move to Austin, Texas, where he would be responsible for managing one of the six offices in the firm. I was thrilled with this new venture and in getting a new home in the process. My world was getting bigger!

Jason would now be going into middle school. Not one of you would dare ask me what I thought about the middle school experience. So I will tell you! Those sweet little kids that you once knew have turned into little monsters! Jason would grow up to be six feet two inches, but he was a very skinny kid. He met his first bully! Jason had never been in a fight in his life.

The bully was in the boys' locker room and started calling Jason by his last name, which was Nicholas, and converting it into a curse word. I know you are wondering how you can take a name like Nicholas and make it into a curse word. However, the bully continued to call Jason this off-color name, and Jason repeatedly asked him to stop, which not only emboldened the bully to continue, but now the other boys in the locker room started doing the same!

Jason didn't tell me for a few weeks because he was really trying to handle this problem himself. His father was out of town, so he brought it to my attention. Now it was up to me to pray and give Jason some advice on what he should do. Jason knew the story of

David and Goliath in the Bible when Goliath was mocking God and what happened (read 1 Samuel chapter 17). I wanted Jason to understand that he carried two names, Nicholas and Christian, both names being honorable and worth fighting for. I simply told Jason, "*Take him out!*" I told him the kid was a bully, and that this behavior would continue if Jason didn't confront him. You don't have to *win* the fight, but you do have to *hurt* him to end this problem! I gave him a few suggestions of my own. I told him that I would be praying for him all day and for Jason to ask God for the *courage* to confront the bully.

I prayed all day until that skinny little boy came walking through the door with a big smile on his face! Sure enough, when he got on the bus, the name-calling started. Jason once again asked the bully to stop, but he just continued, and the fight began—one punch was all that it took! Jason said, "The bus driver had a big smile on his face!" I told Jason that God was with him that day, to thank Him, and to never become a bully himself.

Prayer Truth: We will all face a Goliath at one time or another in this life.

John 16:33 says,

> I have told you these things, so that in Me you may have peace. In this world, you will have trouble. But take heart, I have overcome the world!

Getting Involved in Politics and Interior Design

Politics became something that I would become very interested in, only second to my interest in reading and interior design. Dave and I were involved at a low level in a prior presidential general election and had the privilege to sit on the convention floor for one of our previous presidents. We met a lot of interesting people, many of whom became friends. One couple became lifelong friends. What was unusual about this relationship was that we were not advocates for the same party!

The gentleman was the Chief of Staff and also served as the Postmaster General. One of my greatest honors was that he asked me to give the prayer at his eightieth birthday party.

What did I learn from my brief time in politics? People would lie, lie, lie! For example, we would be on the convention floor listening to various speakers, then rush back to the hotel to see what various news networks would be saying about the speakers. We had just heard the speakers personally, and the news outlets were saying something completely different from what we heard spoken! What they were presenting as *truth* we knew were *lies*! Satan must love politics!

Financial Markets Collapse in the '80s

In Texas and across the country, there was a huge financial collapse. Things were so bad that Dave's company was struggling to the point that he wasn't even giving himself a paycheck. We had to buy our groceries using the small income we were receiving from a rental house we owned. He was really upset when he had to lay off his employees. His company, like many others, was really suffering financially during this recession!

I told him that God was *faithful* in the *good* and *bad* times. I assured him that we would get through this. We had a precious family, we were in good health, we loved one another, and we had a small nest egg in a company in Connecticut. Dave then told me that he had just received a letter from the state of Connecticut informing him that the man with whom Dave had invested his money was now in jail; our money was gone! I asked him, "What are we going to do?"

He reached into his pocket, pulled out a coupon, and said, "Come on, we're going to lunch! Let the good times roll!"

A company in Georgia wanted to buy two of the offices we had left, on the condition that Dave would move to Atlanta. None of us wanted to move to Atlanta, especially Jason. He was getting ready to start high school and did not want to leave his friends. Being the only optimist at this time in the family, I prayed and tried to put a positive spin on the possible move to Atlanta, even if I wasn't feeling it in my heart! We were now visiting Atlanta, staying in a hotel, while we checked out the housing market. We fully well knew it would take a miracle to sell our house in Austin due to the decline in the housing market. During that time, we had a saying, "Would the last one to leave Texas please turn off the lights?"

The first day we were visiting Atlanta was difficult for me. It became apparent that we would have to live a hundred miles outside of Atlanta to be able to buy a home without first selling our home in Austin. The president of the company and his wife were to take us out to dinner that night, so I got dressed and went down to the lobby. Dave and Jason were watching a football game in our room. I was now fighting rebellion and self-pity. Yes, I decided that I would go to the bar and get a drink. The bar was crowded, and everyone was watching the football game and having fun. *So much for that plan*! I then decided to go to the gift shop and buy some cigarettes, except I don't smoke! Finally, I decided to buy a bunch of Snickers candy bars. Then I went down a long hallway to the back of the hotel to gorge myself. There was a fake tree and one chair—perfect! I started stuffing myself with Snickers and having a good cry.

About that time, the back door of the hotel opened, and in came the president of the company and his wife. He walked right up to me, with tears running down my face and a mouth full of Snickers, so I couldn't talk. When I was able to recover somewhat, I asked him not to tell Dave about this event. He agreed, I freshened up, and we all went to dinner. After dinner, they took us back to the hotel. The president gave me a hug and whispered in my ear, "Everything will be fine." They decided to send Dave back to Houston instead of Atlanta. Once again, God had shown us His favor!

Jeremiah 29:11–13 says,

> For I know the plans I have for you, declares the Lord, plans to prosper you and not to harm you, plans to give you hope and a future. Then you will call on Me and come and pray to Me, and I will listen to you. You will seek Me and find Me when you seek Me with all your heart!

Returning to Houston was such a relief and a wonderful experience for all of us. We joined a large church because Jason knew some kids who attended there, and their youth program was excellent.

It was in this church that we would make lifelong relationships with some of the couples in our Sunday School class. We loved that class because it had mixed ages—married couples, divorced men, and women. It made the class feel like a community. I had younger friends, friends my age, and older ones. Our best friends were in that class, and even more important to me was that Dave's best friend was in that class, plus other of his golfing buddies. How can I say thank-you to those who contributed to loving us and enriching our lives?

I learned from this experience that we should always have friends younger and older than ourselves—friends who will encourage you while providing a wealth of knowledge and companionship that will continually bless you.

Prayer Truths:

Iron sharpens iron, and
one man sharpens another.
(Proverbs 27:17)

Therefore, encourage one another as I have loved you! (1 Thessalonians 5:11)

My command is this, that you love one another as I have loved you! (John 15:12)

Carry each other's burdens, and in this way you will fulfill the Laws of Christ! (Galatians 6:2)

Do to others as you would have them do unto you! (Luke 6:31)

Be kind and compassionate to one another, forgiving each other, just as Christ has forgiven you! (Ephesians 4:32)

Jason's Teenage Years

Jason was now going through his teenage years. I remember one summer when you were a counselor for disadvantaged kids at our church's youth camp. You told some hilarious stories about the kids and some of the things they did at camp. I knew that God used you in ways you would not realize until you got to heaven!

I also remembered when you were fifteen and did something that made me so mad that I chased you around the house with a broom. You just started laughing, running upstairs, and I was trying to catch up! When I got to the top of the stairs, you were lying on the floor laughing. I went over to you and gave you a little kick. Then I took my broom and went downstairs.

Another thing I remembered was when you were outside in your bathing suit getting a suntan. I had just walked into the house carrying groceries, and I looked outside only to see you with the largest cigar I had ever seen in your mouth. I simply said, "Son, I want you to finish that entire cigar before you come into the house!" I had never seen you smoke before, and I haven't seen you smoke again!

I remember a time when I was visiting a friend in the hospital, and you asked me if you could take your dad's car for a drive to practice your driving skills. Your dad was out of town; I said no. You said, "You will never know whether I did or not."

I told you, "Oh, yes, I will because when I ask you, you will not lie because you are not a *liar*!"

You were wise beyond your years. I asked you when you were sixteen why you weren't going to the dance. You told me that the girl you wanted to take to the dance was already going with someone else and that you didn't need another girl hanging on your arm just to have a date for the dance. That really impressed your mother!

You were now attending Texas Tech University, located in Lubbock, Texas—nine long hours from Houston! I remember your dad saying that every time you purchased gasoline for your truck, there would be extra charges for snacks and drinks. Your dad took care of those additional expenses!

It wasn't because you didn't like college— it was because you liked it too much! Your grades were excellent except for math. I was so sorry that you inherited the *hate-math gene* from me! While you were in college, you kept changing majors, which meant that you were losing hours/credits, delaying your graduation. Then you received the *Letter to Lubbock* as you referred to it from your dad.

It went something like this: "I realize that you are having a difficult time choosing your major. It had better be resolved quickly! I had better be seeing you receiving your graduation certificate this time next year! Love, Dad!" The night you graduated from Texas Tech was one of the happiest days in your father's life!

You got a job, making good money, and as your father would say, "He is dating every beauty in town!" I even got a letter from one of your girlfriends saying, "Jason really loves me. He just doesn't realize it yet!"

Jason Enters the Marine Corps

You were doing well at work, so when you came home for the weekend and pointed to the *Semper Fi* sticker on the back of your truck, we were stunned! Jason had gone down to a recruiting office of the Marine Corps and signed up to go to Quantico, Virginia, for training as an officer.

You had never mentioned the Marine Corps before—we asked, "Why?"

I remember your exact words: "I want to look back on my life and feel like I had done something worthy." Now our family had plenty of naval officers, but this would be the first Marine. Or as the Marines like to say, "The men's department of the Navy!"

The graduation ceremony for the Marines at Quantico was spectacular! Generals lined up, the military band played, American flags waved, and family and friends were hanging from the rafters. Then the new Marines marched in wearing their uniforms for the first time. Their names and the universities they attended were announced as they were being commissioned. As graduates were leaving the stage floor, their parents would go and greet them. The General patted Jason on his back and said, looking at us, "He has a brilliant career ahead of him." Our buttons were about to burst with pride—then I heard the General say the same thing about the young man following Jason. I looked up at Dave and said, "I'm sure the General was *sincere* when he was talking to us!" The General made me laugh! I thought it was a great line to repeat to each mom and dad.

Jason, two weeks after you were commissioned, 9-11 happened. Your dad and I were out of the country in Quebec, Canada, on a business trip. We, along with all other Americans and Canadians, were in shock! The management of the hotel brought in an American flag, and everyone, including the cooks at the hotel, were in tears as Americans were singing "God Bless America."

Your dad and I immediately called the Marine base, but they were not accepting any calls. The Canadian government shut down all airports, so we couldn't leave the country by air. Your father and another company executive hired a French-speaking Canadian to drive us by bus out of Canada through an illegal route to the United States. I will never forget that trip!

Realizing that our only son would be going to war was a very emotional time. Only people who had sons and daughters in the military would ever understand the impact that this moment had on us!

Later, while you were on your way to the Middle East, an envelope came to the house in the mail addressed to Mr. and Mrs. David Nicholas from the Marine Corps. I opened the envelope and out fell the last will and testament of Lt. Jason David Nicholas. I fell to the floor in fear and immediately told the Lord, "I give my son to You and I ask for his protection!"

Isaiah 26:3 says, "You will keep in perfect peace him whose mind is steadfast because he places his trust in you!" I claimed this Scripture as one of my *life* verses!

It was difficult seeing reports on TV every night concerning this war in the Middle East, knowing that our son was fighting in it. While this war was going on, we had a friend who said that he had seen Jason while he was visiting our troops in Iraq! How grateful we were to have friends in our Sunday school class at church who were praying for our son's protection while he was at war.

Now the war was coming to an end, and we received a letter from you mailed in a Saddam Hussein personal envelope, which I have saved! I framed the envelope from Saddam's personal stationery, embellished with gold, along with the letter from Jason. His grandchildren will treasure this moment that will be a part of their family's history!

"*Howdy, Mom and Dad!*

The First Battalion, Seventh Marines have just seized Saddam Hussein's presidential palace. This morning, I am standing on Saddam's balcony overlooking the Tigris and Euphrates rivers, smoking one of Saddam's Cuban cigars."

Jason informed us that he got to see the Hanging Gardens, one of the wonders of the ancient world. He also told us that he saw the room where Nebuchadnezzar's son Belshazzar drank from God's gold goblets while praising other gods. That is when suddenly a human hand appeared and wrote on the plaster of the wall. You can read the entire story in Daniel 5.

Divine Intervention

He told us about a particular mission that the Marines had taken when there was no moon. Six Humvees in the desert without a moon proved to be a real blessing from the Lord. One of the Humvees rolled over on a deep sand hill, so they stopped the convoy to make sure everyone was okay. Out of the darkness, a soldier walked up to the Colonel and said, "Why are you here?" He continued, "You need to leave immediately because ahead of you is a Saddam tank brigade!" The soldier then walked back into the darkness, and the Colonel said to his men, "That was divine providence!" They never saw the soldier again.

I could go on and on, but I won't. However, I truly believe that God performs miracles in our lives without us always recognizing them. There are no words to describe how a parent feels when they get the news that their son or daughter is coming home. It is exhilarating and humbling to realize that God has protected your child in a very difficult situation (war). But we must always remember the soldiers and their families of the ones who didn't make it home or came home severely injured.

We had intended to fly to California to welcome Jason home, but Jason told us that he would fly directly into Houston a few days later. He wanted to first visit his men who had been hospitalized from the injuries they had received while serving with Jason in the war. We had a great greeting for him when he arrived at Houston Intercontinental Airport and then had a wonderful party later to celebrate his homecoming!

I memorized the entire chapter of Psalm 91 while Jason was in the war in Iraq. Every day, I would pray it over our military. I knew that God's angels were there to protect them. I sincerely believe, with all my heart, that the soldier who came out of the darkness and spoke to the Colonel was an angel!

> If you make the "Most High" your dwelling—even the Lord who is my refuge— no harm shall befall you, no disaster will come near your tent. For He will command His angels concerning you to guard you in all your ways; they will lift you up in their hands, so that you will not strike your foot against a stone. (Psalm 91:9–12)

Have you noticed that life is a continuation of struggles and peace? When facing struggles, as Christians, we realize that God is our only hope. However, when the struggle is over—often, so are our prayers. Don't let that happen!

When you come to realize that God is sovereign and in complete control of everything—and I mean everything—you will never look at the world or the people who live in the world as though they have the answers to life's issues. Remember that we are all flawed and have a sinful nature except for our Lord and Savior Jesus Christ!

Just as I had given Jason to God when he went off to war, never did I dream I would experience again the truth of Your Word.

> You keep in perfect
> peace him whose mind is
> steadfast because he trusts in
> You. (Isaiah 26:3)

Jason just learned at the age of forty-six that he needed open-heart surgery. I knew that the first thought he would have was remembering that his father had died of a heart condition.

I immediately called all the prayer warriors at church, those in my Bible study group, and all our friends to pray for God to bless Jason with a successful heart surgery. It was touch and go for a few weeks, but God was faithful and completely healed Jason's heart! Now I want to ask you, who will you call on when a crisis comes into your life? Crisis will come to all of us while we are here on earth. No one will leave this earth without having to face struggles of some kind.

> I have told you these things so that in Me you may have peace. In this world you will have trouble, but take courage, I have

overcome the world. (John 16:33)

Find rest, oh my soul, in God alone; my hope comes from Him. He alone is my rock and my salvation; He is my fortress, I will never be shaken. My salvation and honor depend on God; He is my mighty rock, my refuge. Trust in Him at all times, O people; pour out your hearts to Him, for God is our refuge. (Psalm 62:5–8)

Prayer Truth: Prayers can release our tensions in times of emotional stress. Trusting God to be our rock and fortress will change our entire outlook on life! We no longer need to be held captive by having resentment toward someone who hurt us. When we are resting in God's strength, nothing can shake us!

A few years passed, which were happy and content years for our family. The next major change in our lives was when Dave received a call from DFW International Airport, making Dave a job offer he couldn't refuse. We both loved our church and the friends we had made in Houston, but the weather in Houston, not so much! The plan was for Dave to finish his commitment to DFW International Airport and then retire. We both loved to travel, and retirement would allow us to take trips with no restrictions because of Dave having to work, work, work!

We were busy making plans as to where we would live in the Dallas/Fort Worth Metroplex. We decided to live in Colleyville, which is located near DFW International Airport. Dave moved into an apartment and started setting up the teams he would need for the airport project. I stayed behind in

Houston, getting our home ready to sell, organizing the many details that come with moving, finishing up my personal commitments, and spending time saying goodbye to my precious friends.

We did have one special experience while living on South Post Oak Street in Houston. Just down the street from us was where President George H. W. Bush and his wife, Barbara, lived. It had its benefits because whenever there was a thunderstorm in Houston that would knock out the power throughout the city, we seemingly would always have power on our street.

There was a particular restaurant on that street that maintained a low profile, and we tried to keep it quiet so tourists wouldn't find it. One weekend, when Jason was on leave from the Marines, we decided to go there for a late lunch. The first thing I did was go into the ladies' room and mess with my hair. While I was in the ladies' restroom, I missed out on all the action! As it turned out, the Bushes, too, had decided to have a late lunch, and President Bush walked over to our table and said to Jason, "I would know a Marine anywhere," and they had a brief conversation.

When I came out of the restroom, Dave told me what happened. Then Dave said to me, "Don't you dare look in their direction—let them eat their lunch in peace!" Of course, I *took a peek* at them, and Barbara was kind enough to give me a wave. I promise I did not look at them again!

Dave selected a contractor to build our new home. Now as far as the apartment was concerned, remember I told you that Dave was Welsh—he wasn't about to spend a lot of money sprucing it up for just a short period of time. It was a cold November day when I saw our love nest, which is what I decided to call it. When the door opened, about twenty leaves blew into the apartment with us. I stomped on the leaves and told Dave, "Don't worry, sweetheart. No one will notice them in this shag carpet for twenty years." Dave had ordered some furniture that had a '60s look: a table, four chairs, and a couch, which I can't even describe. The fake palm tree was bent in half, and he had electrical wires taped to the shag carpet with all lines connected to his computer and some other equipment…very charming!

I didn't know it then, but this would be our last winter together. In the hall closet were our washer and dryer. They were about six steps from where our shower was in our apartment. I would warm up a towel for Dave while he was taking a shower, and when I heard the shower stop, I would remove the towel from the dryer and throw the warm towel over to him so he could have a warm towel to dry on. He would yell, "You get an extra ten points for doing that!"

Now why would that memory be so precious to me? So simple, but that message said to Dave, "I love you!" Maybe this expression of love will speak to your heart and challenge you to create ways to express your love to people who are special to you.

> By this, everyone will
> know you are my disciples
> by my love. (John 13:35)

I remember one morning looking around the apartment and having the strangest thought: *How would I feel if Dave came home and told me that he had lost his job and that we would be living in this apartment permanently?* I looked up at the *popcorn ceiling* and thought, *I had better start scraping it if this is going to be my permanent home!* I know in my heart that between us, we would have made it adorable! Our first home was in an attic apartment, and we worked hard to make it look great in our eyes!

Prayer Truth:

> I know what it is to be in
> need, and I know what it is
> to have plenty. I have learned
> the secret of being content
> in any and every situation,
> whether well-fed or hungry,
> whether living in plenty or
> in want. (Philippians 4:12)

We all have asked God for things that we want in this life. I certainly have, but I realized an *amazing truth* whenever I said, "Lord, I want what You want me to have." I have always received a greater abundance of His blessings than anything I could have ever imagined!

It was in this apartment where we lived while our home was being built. During this time, I became involved in an international Bible study in Grapevine, Texas. Again, God blessed me with many *sisters in Christ* through this organization.

The house was finally completed, and we were so excited about moving into it. Moving day at last! The movers brought in the last box and left. Then Dave went and sat in his office chair and said, "I don't feel well." For Dave to say that caused my heart to start pounding because I felt that something was terribly wrong! I was getting ready to call 911, but Dave said, "No, take me to the hospital." I didn't even know where the hospital was located. I had one name and phone number of a person in my Bible study group. I immediately called her because I knew that she lived close to our new home. Little did I know that Dave would not spend one night in our new home!

The lady that I called was there in a flash, and we went immediately to the emergency room at the hospital in Grapevine, Texas. The doctor told me that Dave's heart was failing and they were going to do an emergency procedure on him. I immediately called my best friend in Houston, and she came quickly to be with me. Word soon spread, and my new friends from Bible study and our new church surrounded me.

I wasn't alone; God knew exactly what was happening. Jason, who was now a Captain, had left the Marine Corps and become a student at the Southwestern Baptist Seminary in Fort Worth, Texas. God, in His wisdom, had brought me to Dallas/Fort Worth because my son was here! Of course, Jason was a major source of my strength while I was going through those three difficult days.

Nothing more could be done to save him. We knew Dave was dying. The nurses rushed into the room to make him comfortable. I just started thanking him for being such a wonderful husband and father, thanking him with words that were special between the two of us.

Our friends from Houston were praying for us. I felt those prayers, and they truly sustained me. Dave's best friend and golfing partner had come to the hospital from Houston and was able to tell Dave goodbye. He also told him that they would be playing golf together again one day in heaven!

I then asked everyone to leave the room because I wanted to be with Dave for a little longer by myself. I'm so glad that I did. When I looked at him, I knew his spirit had departed to be with the Lord. I kissed him, told him that I loved him, and then I said goodbye. God uses grief in different ways. For weeks, through God's grace, I was in a cocoon of peace. Then my grief would change to heartache because God would use this time to grow my dependence and trust in the Lord.

When everyone had left, Jason stayed with me for weeks. I can't remember exactly how long he stayed. He was a huge blessing, encouraging me and doing all the things that needed to be done, especially after the head of the house had died. He even got me the best insurance plan ever! He insisted that I get a new car so he wouldn't have to worry about my safety.

I had never heard of a company named OnStar, but they provide driving directions to anywhere I might be going. Jason had that service installed in my new car. I guess Jason knew that I could get lost in a parking lot! Therefore, he said to me, "Mom, you are now living in a new town, and you don't know where you are going!" I would probably have been asking total strangers for directions to get me home. His *mission* was now accomplished! He would now leave and return to his home.

My first night alone after Dave died was the first time in my life that I understood the unbelievable blessing of having a heavenly Father. My emotions were everywhere! I was in grief, scared, worried, full of anxiety, and alone.

I just unloaded on the Lord—I didn't have twenty years to make new friends! I didn't even have a doctor, dentist, or any other emergency contact. I went to the grocery store and had a crying breakdown because I couldn't find the green beans. A lady in the store walked over to comfort me. I really think that she was an angel, and she helped me find the green beans. During the early days of this major change in my life, I just kept calling out to the Lord to help me!

Prayer Truth: Prayer can release our tension and anxiety during times of emotional stress. Trusting God to be our rock, salvation, and fortress will change our entire outlook on life!

Not only did He find me a doctor who said that he was not taking any additional patients, but He also found me a dentist!

Why Friendships Matter

First, you need to be a good friend. God absolutely opened the circumstances of finding good friends for me. I realized that I needed to ask God for everything. I wanted to make sure that He did the picking because He knows every heart!

Prayer Truth: In life, you will have two different circles of friends. There is a small circle of friends who become lifelong friends, then there are people with whom you interface frequently—some are friends for an extended period of time and some are friends for just a season.

> A man of many com-
> panions may come to ruin,
> but there is a friend that
> sticks closer than a brother.
> (Proverbs 18:24)

The greatest friend that any one of us will ever have on this earth is Jesus!

My best friends are those who love Jesus with all their hearts, minds, souls, and strength. I was a widow for many years, and it was these friends who were always there for me physically, emotionally, and spiritually!

I had three serious illnesses during this period, and I am amazed that I am still alive! The Bible says that people would typically live for seventy years and maybe eighty years. Lord, for the record, *I have exceeded my expiration date!* I prayed that the Lord would keep me fresh and green so I could bear fruit for His glory! I have had an extended life by the *grace* of God! I had to laugh one time when one of my friends said she thought for sure that COVID would do me in! I thought that comment was hilarious!

I remember two things about being in the hospital with COVID. The first was when I heard two nurses talking and one said, "Look, she is breathing on her own!" The second memory was in the middle of the night when a nurse came into my room wearing plastic clothing with a large round clear helmet on her head, and I asked her, "Are we on Mars?"

Through all these health challenges, I would run to the *cross* in my mind, and I wouldn't let go! This is why memorizing Scripture is so important. Remember, God's Word is your *sword*—you don't have to swing it; you just have to speak it!

> I have hidden your
> word in my heart that I
> might not sin against you.
> (Psalm 119:11)

Prayer Partners

In Jesus's time, women would meet at the well not only to draw water but to have fellowship with one another. This example continues today with women getting together to have a cup of coffee or lunch. This type of fellowship in the Christian community often leads to discussions about the Bible and, as a result, the ladies desire to have a deeper relationship with Jesus.

The problem is that women like to talk, and when they find themselves alone while they pray, they sometimes feel like they are not getting a response from God. It can feel like playing tennis when you hit the ball over the net and it doesn't come back to you.

Counting one, two, three, four, five, six, seven, eight, nine… Is the ball ever going to come back over the net?

Prayer Truths:

> Call to me and I will answer you, telling you unsearchable things that you do not know. (Jeremiah 33:3)

> For where two or three come together in my name, there am I with them. (Matthew 18:20)

How magnificent that our God is telling us, especially women, to pour out our hearts to Him. No one on this earth can do that but Jesus! Sometimes I wonder if He put cotton in His ears because when I start pouring out my prayer requests to Him, I don't hear anything coming back from Him. But *surprise*! The Lord will answer every one of those prayers in His perfect timing!

Having a prayer partner or belonging to a prayer group means that the tennis ball is coming back. We get to have fellowship with Jesus and with one another at the same time!

Over the years, I have had many prayer partners, and each one of them helped me grow spiritually while praying and studying God's Word together. Having had a prayer ministry for many years gave me the opportunity to mentor many women in teaching them how to pray. They learned that there is power in prayer and that it is simply a two-way communication between them and their heavenly Father!

> Ask and it will be given
> to you, seek and you will
> find; knock and the door
> will be opened to you. For

everyone who asks receives; the one who seeks finds; and to the one who knocks, the door will be opened. (Matthew 7:7–8)

Families Matter

We all have families, but the problem is we didn't get the opportunity to pick them out! We inherited them through birth, marriage, and possibly adoption. So there will be an assortment of personalities, nationalities, cultures, and faiths. As a result, there may be family members that you wish weren't a part of your life!

You will have a father, a mother, brothers and sisters, aunts, uncles, cousins, and it goes on and on! Your children get married, and now you have a son-in-law or daughter-in-law; now there are outlaws. I think you understand what I am saying. The only ones that come out *perfect in our eyes* are the grandchildren!

You will have family members that will enrich your life and you can't wait to see them! And you will have family members that you can't wait to see go!

Prayer Truth: You can't expect people to be what they aren't or to give you what they don't possess! There will be family members that you so badly want to connect with, but it just doesn't happen. However, you will find that praying for them will provide you much comfort and peace—we must let go of them and let God do His work!"

Guess what? God put each one of them in your life for His purpose. For example, I had a fantastic father-in-law, but a mother-in-law. I want to show *grace*, so I will just say that she was very difficult. After my father-in-law died, we of course took care of Dave's mother. But just to give you an idea of what I was dealing with, she was asked to leave two very nice senior living establishments.

Being a Christian, God was testing me to show her compassion and love, which I sincerely tried to do. However, I was a complete failure! I was the one who took her to doctor appointments, to her hairdresser, to her favorite restaurants, and everywhere else in between. I did try to share Jesus with her, but she wasn't interested! Challenging is an understatement. I prayed every time I left my home, before picking her up, that the Lord would give me a special love for my mother-in-law and that the day would go well! Within ten minutes, my heart was filled with anger!

After my mother-in-law died, we went to dinner with some friends, and they started telling me how impressed they were with the loving way I had treated her. I told them about the thoughts that I had and that I didn't deserve their praise. My friend's husband placed his hand on top of mine and said, "At least you didn't kill her!"

In God's eyes, *what you think is just as important as what you do!*

> For I know that nothing good dwells in me, that is, in my flesh. For I have the desire to do what is right, but not the ability to carry it out. (Romans 7:18)

Who we really are is in our thought life. We are truly what we think! That is why this stinking thinking must be immediately addressed by confessing that sin to God and asking for His forgiveness!

So what did I learn from this experience? Whenever I would get a daughter-in-law, I would be good to her, loving and respecting her, and supporting her in whatever way she needed! Little did I know that very soon

Jason would meet his wife in Sunday school. It seems that all the girls would come and greet Jason in class, but Chelsea paid him little to no attention. Smart girl!

One of my favorite stories about Chelsea is her ability to shoot a gun! Here is a girl that you would never expect to be a hunter! She is beautiful, delicate in her appearance, and very quiet in her nature! Jason is very proud of his shooting skills. So where does Jason choose to take her on their first date? To a shooting range! He proceeded to show off his shooting skills. Now it was Chelsea's turn—she blew him completely out of the water! It turns out that Chelsea's father owns a safari company, and she had traveled with him many times on hunting expeditions all over the world. She had previously won an award in Africa, from Safari Club International, as the "Best Young Hunter of 2004." Needless to say, Chelsea was the right girl for him!

On November 10, 2012, they were married. It was a beautiful wedding in the Hill Country located in Central Texas. Their wedding was on the same day that the Marine Corps celebrated their birthday—*once a Marine, always a Marine!* I was so grateful for this beautiful young woman who married my son. She is a wonderful wife and mother!

I was in my seventies, waiting for my first grandchild. It was quite humorous to me that my friends who were twenty years younger than me were also waiting for their first grandchild. We would be pushing our baby carriages together!

It took many years to finally have a child, and to experience the joy of being a *Grammie* was so thrilling! I had prayed previously to the Lord that He would not allow a child to be born in the Nicholas family who would not know Jesus Christ as their Savior. Why did I pray this? Because when a person dies, they will either go to heaven or to hell! That decision will be the biggest decision they will ever make in their life. You are given the gift of eternal life by believing that Jesus is the Son of God, that He died on the cross for our sins, and that He was resurrected on the third day from the grave. If you don't accept this gift, you will be singing the song "I Did It My Way" on your way to hell!

Please read the following scriptures in the Book of Matthew: Matthew 13:42, 13:50, and 25:46.

My prayers were answered by God giving Chelsea to Jason as his wife. I now never had to worry! This child would grow up in a home where both parents were devout Christians!

On December 9, 2017, Jody Olivia Nicholas was born. I realized that every grandparent thought their grandchild was the best—well—sorry to tell all the other grandparents, but the most beautiful, gifted, kind-hearted, smartest little girl ever born is mine!

Oh Jody, when you are all grown up and reading this testimony, I pray that you will remember how much your Grammie loved you! The fun times that we had together and the family vacations that we took together! But most of all, I wanted you to remember that your Grammie prayed for you every day!

I wanted you to remember when you spent the night at Grammie's house, I would start each morning saying, "Good morning, God. Good morning, Jesus. Good morning, Holy Spirit, I surrender all! I give You my will!"

You always provided our entertainment. I had so many stories and memories to share about you, but that would take another book to cover them all. Therefore, I will share with you two of my favorites.

When you were four years old taking swimming lessons, you noticed a little girl who had no hair. You asked your mother why the little girl didn't have any hair. Your mama told you that the little girl had to wear a beautiful wig because her body couldn't grow hair. You were silent and thought for a short period of time, then you looked up at your mama and said, "I think that Daddy has that disease!"

Another favorite memory that I had of you was one time when you were spending the night at Grammie's. I slept in your bed with you so that you would feel secure. In the middle of the night, you woke me up by lifting up one of my eyelids and saying, "Grammie, you are snoring. You need to go and sleep on the couch!" So I took a pillow and a blanket and went to the couch. A few minutes later, here you came bringing me a stuffed animal, and you said, "Here, Grammie, I don't want you to sleep alone!"

Your parents built a new home on ten acres of land, which gave you plenty of room to play outside and explore the surroundings, which was one of your favorite things to do. Your world got bigger now that you were going to school and taking horseback riding lessons. We were excited to recently meet the new member of your family, a darling Maremma puppy named Emma! Also, I understood that you helped build the chicken coop where your four chickens lived, named Pork Chop, Macaroni, Bronco, and Lucy!

You are seven years old, and I knew that time would go fast over the next few years! So, I hid every memory of you deep in my *heart*, and I never forgot God's goodness and grace in giving me such a wonderful granddaughter as you! God wanted us to witness and minister to our families first!

Chocolate Ice Cream Soda with a Cherry on Top

I was ready for a change in my life! I had been living alone in my beautiful home for so many years, and I was lonely. I heard about a new senior living community being built near where I lived in Colleyville, Texas. So I decided that I would sell my home after that facility was built and move into it. This would provide me with a whole new adventure in my life. But it wasn't to be!

Enters J. C. Matlock into my life. He didn't have a regular name, just initials. J.C.

was a neighbor who lived across the street. I didn't interact much with my neighbors, so I didn't really know him. All I knew about him was that he was a good caregiver to his sick wife for years and that he was now a widower.

One summer day, there was a knock at my front door, and there stood J.C. with a cantaloupe and a couple of vine-ripened tomatoes. It appeared that J. C. had been to the local farmer's market and bought enough to share with others in the neighborhood!

The next day, I was going out to my mailbox and yelled to J. C., who was working in his yard, that I had just eaten the best tomato sandwich I had eaten in years. So our love relationship began! I had been a widow for ten years and had no desire to date or get married again. When someone would ask me why I wasn't interested in having a relationship with a man, I would simply say that I was looking for Jesus with skin on! God must have a sense of humor! When my friends learned that I was dating a man named "J. C.," they just started laughing.

I didn't want him coming into my house, and I wouldn't go into his either. We would just meet under a large tree near our homes. J. C. thought this was ridiculous! One weekend, I went on a girlfriend's trip, and when I finally arrived home that night, my cell phone was dead! So I went over to J. C.'s house in the rain to see if he could fix my phone. He invited me into his house so he could look at my phone to determine what was wrong with it. I looked around at this spotlessly clean and charming home, where the only thing out of place was a blood pressure device sitting on his couch. He had just taken his blood pressure before I had come over. So I asked him to take my blood pressure. He said, "Rene, you realize that our neighbors are thinking that some *wild and crazy* things are going on over at J. C.'s house, and here we are taking our blood pressure!"

We progressed from that night to going to church together, going to dinner together, and walking periodically in the park! I found him to be smart, quick-witted, and one good-looking guy! He had asked me to marry him a couple of times while we were walking at the park, but I was waiting for the Holy Spirit to give me the *green* light that it was okay for us to get married. I remember J. C. asking me what I was afraid of, and I told him about our health and our age. He said to me, "Rene, we're not getting any younger, and God has a day for us to be born and a day for us to die!" He said, "God is sovereign and in control!"

J. C. had been successful throughout his life. He received his business administration degree from the University of Houston while working full-time at Exxon as a computer operator. After leaving Exxon, he became responsible for global computer operations for The Coca-Cola Company. While working at The Coca-Cola Company, he was given the opportunity to represent Coke in the Atlanta Golf Classic Pro/AM, where he played with Jack Nicklaus. Jack beat him by one stroke! J. C. could have been a professional golfer. He left The Coca-Cola Company and became the executive vice president for a consulting company. Later in his career, he founded a computer security firm and took it public! The name of the company was Total Assets Protection, Inc., and it became the darling of Wall Street. Throughout his career, he was closely associated with computers!

Obviously, I really respected what he had accomplished in his life, but what really impressed me was how he lived his life: God, family, and career. For example, every week that the garbage truck would come by my house to pick up my trash, someone would take my trash containers from the curb and put them up next to my garage. This went on for eight years before I found out that it was

J. C. who was doing it! He would also give Gatorade to the men picking up the garbage.

He was selected to be a deacon at his church, and he invited me to attend the ordination service. I could see how respected he was by that church's congregation. The spiritual connection was what really attracted him to me.

I said yes to marrying J. C. on April 4, 2020. Because of COVID, we had to be married on J.C.'s beautiful patio, where only ten people were allowed to attend the wedding. It was a lovely wedding with only immediate family members in attendance.

He makes me laugh and treats me like every woman would like to be treated by their husbands! Jesus blessed me again by giving me a gift beyond measure, my beloved J. C.!

So how do I end this testimony?

I will come and proclaim Your mighty acts, O

Sovereign Lord; I will proclaim Your righteousness,
You alone. Since my youth,
O God, You have taught
me, and to this day I declare
Your marvelous deeds. Even
when I am old and gray, do
not forsake me O God, till
I declare Your power to the
next generation, Your might
to all who are to come.
(Psalm 71:16–18)

www.ingramcontent.com/pod-product-compliance
Lightning Source LLC
Chambersburg PA
CBHW022012150726
47990CB00002B/629